D1169200

CARD *for* GAMES
SMART KIDS

Margie Golick, Ph.D.

**Official
American Mensa
Game Book**

STERLING PUBLISHING CO., INC.
New York

For Marlee Samantha

American revision edited by Jeanette Green
Card game selection by Peter Gordon
Designed by Jeff Fitschen & Illustrated by Jane Churchill

Library of Congress Cataloging-in-Publication Data
Golick, Margie.
  Card games for smart kids / Margie Golick.
    p.   cm.
  Includes index.
  Summary: Presents descriptions of and directions for more than
forty card games
    ISBN 0-8069-4887-6
    1. Card games—Juvenile literature. [1. Card games. 2. Games.]
  I. Title.
GV1244.G65 1998
795.4—dc21   98-30848

3   5   7   9   10   8   6   4

Published by Sterling Publishing Company, Inc.
387 Park Avenue South, New York, N.Y. 10016
© 1998 by Margie Golick
Portions were previously published by
Pembroke Publishers Ltd., Markham, Ontario,
in *Reading, Writing, and Rummy* © 1986 by Margie Golick.
Distributed in Canada by Sterling Publishing
% Canadian Manda Group, One Atlantic Avenue, Suite 105
Toronto, Ontario, Canada M6K 3E7
Distributed in Great Britain and Europe by Cassell PLC
Wellington House, 125 Strand, London WC2R 0BB, England
Distributed in Australia by Capricorn Link (Australia) Pty Ltd.
P.O. Box 6651, Baulkham Hills, Business Centre, NSW 2153, Australia
Manufactured in the United States of America
All rights reserved

Sterling ISBN 0-8069-4887-6

CONTENTS

Acknowledgments

I have been playing cards with children for more than forty years. In that time, I've had an opportunity to play cards with children from all over the world, especially in Canada, the United States, Australia, New Zealand, Israel, Barbados, and Trinidad. Even here at home in Montreal, children from many countries have enriched my repertoire of card games. Many of them are now grown-up, but I remember them all fondly. I am grateful to them and to friends, relatives, and colleagues who have taught me some of their favorite games or played a few hands with me to help me refine the playing rules. I am especially grateful now to my grandchildren James, Alex, Suzannah, and Lena, who are all still enthusiastic card players.

CARD SMARTS

"I am sorry I have not learned to play at cards. It is very useful in life; it generates kindness and consolidates society."
— Dr. Samuel Johnson (1709–1784)

I have been hanging around playing cards all my life. One of my earliest childhood memories is of sitting under a table entertaining myself with a handful of jokers while my parents and their friends played bridge atop the table.

My grandparents taught me the first card games I ever played—War and Go Fish. Later they taught me Casino and 500 Rummy. And as I got older, I spent hours on weekend afternoons playing Hearts and Whist with my friends in a small Nova Scotia town.

When I grew up and began to teach and counsel children, many kids taught me new games, tricks, and tips for play. Slowly I became a kind of expert, if not a card shark. And I rediscovered what a friendly skill card playing is.

It is a wonderful rainy-day activity that I often enjoyed with my own children and that I'm now playing with my grandchildren. It's great to break out the cards when you decide you want a little challenge or sociability. You can play at home on the living-room floor, on the kitchen table, in the car on trips, in the train, on airplanes, or in waiting rooms. Or take them to the farm or a country cottage.

In my own card-playing family, children can play a few games by age four, and they gradually expand their repertoire year by year. Kids under four like to have cards to carry around to play in imitation of older brothers and sisters. Sometimes they make up their own rules or change rules in the middle of a game. After a while, they learn that what makes a game a game is that it has rules everyone follows.

When you learn to play cards, there are lots of useful things you can learn. But the most important thing is to have fun. Adults can get carried away and try to make what could be a delightful game into a flash-card kind of drill. Make sure your card playing really is a game and that it's fun. In a good card game, your hands, eyes, and mind are all busy. Rules must be remembered and followed. All players are equal, whether adult or child, and there are winners and losers. In card games and solitaire, there is an element of suspense because the outcome is unpredictable. It's the result of skill, luck, or both.

A deck of cards is an amazing invention. Just think about it! Cards from a standard deck can be divided in many ways—into red and black; suits (clubs, diamonds, hearts, and spades); and denominations (aces, twos, threes, etc.). The number cards (ace through ten) can be separated from the face cards, and the face cards, in turn, can be divided into men (jacks and kings) and women (queens). Within the suits the numbers make it possible to order the cards from low to high or high to low.

Also, you can do things with the numbers printed on the cards—add, subtract, or multiply them. A standard deck has 52 cards, plus a couple of jokers. The deck can be handed out and divided in various ways. Hundreds of card games exist because they make use of the many characteristics of cards. In your deck, you may be able to divide face cards into figures facing left and figures facing right. Also, figures may be in profile while others appear full-face. Other figures may have swords and still others battle-axes.

Modern cards are also flexible, which allows us to rearrange them and mix them up by shuffling them. They are fun to hold and often pretty to look at.

You may enjoy collecting cards from other countries and places you or thoughtful friends travel. Souvenir cards often have scenes on the front or back. And some cards have suit markings that reflect local traditions. In Germany, hearts, bells, acorns, and leaves replace the usual hearts, diamonds, clubs, and spades. In Spain and Portugal, the suits are swords, batons, coins, and cups. In Switzerland you'll find shields, bells, acorns, and flowers. You may also find letters that abbreviate the names of court cards in the language of the country, like the French *R* or *roi* for "king," *D* or *dame* for "queen," and *V* or *valet* for "jack."

Other cards may bear Russian, Arabic, or Chinese script. I've found a deck designed by an artist in which each card is very different, beautiful, and surprising. I've also seen funny decks and decks that collect interesting facts. Others display animals, trees, wildflowers, lovely women, handsome men, movie stars, politicians, airplanes, famous paintings, and even stay-fit exercises and 1,200-calorie diets.

Advertisers also produce card decks, stamping a commercial message on the back or front. My father, who owned a shoe store, found a deck that contained virtually a whole catalog of shoes, since each card described a shoe and its price. Most of these advertising decks can be used for play since they also contain suits and numbers in the small corners.

Jumbo cards can be used to demonstrate card games to a group. And tiny ones fit small hands. I've also seen teeny ones made for doll houses. Round decks can be fun, or they can be used, as my mother once suggested, for coasters.

This book contains a collection of card games and solitaires I've collected in my travels and at home. Included are games for beginners, games for experienced players, and games for people of all ages and card-playing abilities that can be enjoyed together. Back-Alley Bridge is fun for players from five to ninety-five.

Card games also help us sharpen many skills. If you like math, or even if you don't, card games can make math fun. Try Knuckles, Finders Keepers, Creights, Odds and Evens, Hit the Mark, and more. If you're quick with visual details, or want to be, or if you just want to show off, try Speed. Terrific for those with a good memory are Kings, Hit the Mark, and Nine—Five—Two. Coffee Pot demands deduction. And the card games Sentence Rummy and Alliteration play with language and vocabulary.

Also, when you explain the rules of a card game to

friends, you'll need to be clear and precise. You'll find yourself saying cue words like *first, then, before, after, under, over, behind, between, above, below.*

Card games engage players in classifying, ordering, reasoning, deducing, and devising strategies to solve a problem. These same skills help in science, math, and other studies. They help us concentrate, focus attention, hone motor skills (shuffling, dealing, and fanning cards), and become more sociable.

You'll enjoy playing the many games in this book. Also, try to expand your repertoire and knowledge of what cards offer. Ask other kids from other regions and countries to teach you games. Ask adults to teach you games they know. You'll find many similarities in games from around the world.

Cards are great ice-breakers with others who perhaps don't speak English yet. Kids with physical disabilities, like hearing loss or visual impairment, can play cards, since one need not hear to play and Braille decks are available. It's also fun to play with everyone from senior citizens to children you baby-sit or, indeed, with your own babysitter or nanny.

A deck of cards can be a wonderful gift, with or without a book of rules for games—though we recommend this one! It's also fun to play cards at birthday parties, whether it's with kids only or aunts and uncles are permitted to join. You can set tables for two, four, or more with cards and colored counters. Have players move from table to table, and have adults or someone available to teach games to kids who want to learn. You can make prizes and favors with different decks of cards. Miniature cards are valued favors. You can have refreshments—like sandwiches, raw veggies, cookies, or candies—in the shape of clubs, diamonds, hearts, and spades. You can even send out invitations on old, incomplete decks.

At one card party, we had a fortune-teller, since certain fortune-telling decks have been used at least since the Middle Ages. But this was all in fun; no one was meant to believe the fantastic future told. (I'd be cautious here with the gullible, though.)

Here's an important tip. Harvard mathematicians say that seven ordinary shuffles are necessary to guarantee that cards are thoroughly mixed. So, learn how to shuffle the cards well. You can also show off, if you like. The riffle shuffle sounds nice and looks pretty—in the right hands. Shuffling between dealing cards guarantees that at each deal players begin on equal footing. And avoid that clever little girl, like Maddy, who greets you with cards but warns that you're not going to shuffle for this game. Of course, she wins with all the aces.

SOLITAIRES

Having a stock of solitaire games is a useful diversion when you need to do something with your hands, eyes, and mind.

I have never met a game of solitaire I didn't like. There is something very satisfying in starting with disorder—a random arrangement of cards—and watching order restored, as the cards fall into a special pattern, change places according to a plan, or form an ordered sequence from ace through king.

GRANDMA'S SOLITAIRE

Ages: 6 to adult

Layout

Deal four faceup cards in a square.

Value of Cards

Aces are high.

Object of the Game

The object of the game Grandma's Solitaire is to remove cards and to be left with only the four aces.

Play

If two or more faceup cards are of the same suit, remove the lower card(s). Deal four more cards, covering the cards in the layout or the spaces that remain. After each deal, whenever there are cards of the same suit, always remove the cards lower in value. If a space becomes available, the top card of any pile may be used to fill the space. Before dealing the next four cards, always check for possible removals. Deal out all the cards. The game is won when only the four aces remain.

Learning Skills

• classification • relative value of numbers

PLUS OR MINUS ONE

Ages: 5 to adult

Object of the Game

The object of the game Plus or Minus One is to build all the cards into a single pile by playing cards (regardless of suit) that are one higher or one lower than the faceup card. For instance, if the faceup card is a four, either a three or a five may be played on it. A king may be played on an ace and an ace on a king.

Point Value of Cards

Cards ace through ten all have face value.
Jack = 11
Queen = 12
King = 13

Play

Hold the deck facedown and deal the top card faceup to the table to start the "build." Turn up cards one at a time. If the turned-up card is one less or one greater than the faceup "build" card, it is played faceup on the pile. If not, it is played to a discard pile. Play continues until all cards are dealt out. Then the discard pile is turned over and play resumed.

The official rules call for two additional deals of the deck. Since the game is seldom won in this version, I have modified it. I allow unlimited deals until no more plays can be made. When a game is won, count the number of run-throughs of the deck it took. When the game is lost, count how many cards are left in the discard pile. By keeping track of how many times the deck has been dealt for wins and how many leftovers for losses, a child will have an interesting record, as well as many opportunities to learn by heart the result of adding or subtracting one to the numbers from 2 to 13.

PLUS OR MINUS TWO

This is played exactly like Plus or Minus One, except that the increment between cards is 2. Thus, on a 6 you may play an 8 or a 4; on a 3, an A or a 5. On a queen, you may play a 10 (– 2) or an ace (+ 2); on a king you may play a jack (– 2) or a 2 (+ 2).

For children who are adept at arithmetic, or for those who want to develop computational skill, the possibilities are obvious: Plus or Minus Three, Plus or Minus Four, Plus or Minus Five.

Learning Skills

• addition and subtraction

> One writer on cards states that *ace* means "money," and that the card is traditionally more valuable than the king in card games because the king would be powerless without money. Another account explains that, during the Renaissance, society came to realize that the king exists to serve the people. Therefore, the lowest common man is more powerful than the king, and in cards the ace takes precedence over the king.

SEVENS

Equipment

A deck of cards.

Object of the Game

The object of the game Sevens is to get rid of all the cards.

Point Value of Cards

Ace to 10 equal their face value.
Jack = 11 points
Queen = 12 points
King = 13 points

Play

Deal cards in a row. Remove, as they are laid faceup, sevens and all adjacent cards that total any multiple of seven.

Learning Skills

• addition and multiplication (7 times table)

NINES

Ages: 6 to adult

This is a good addition to anybody's repertoire of solitaires that provide practice in computation. If the young player doesn't know number facts by heart, provide a key—a sheet of paper with the needed sums written out (8 + 1 = 9; 7 + 2 = 9; 6 + 3 = 9; 5 + 4 = 9).

After a few deals of Nines, even a chronic forgetter of number facts will memorize the combinations of numbers that equal nine.

Equipment

A deck of cards.

Layout

Deal nine faceup cards in three rows of three.

Play

Cover, with faceup cards from the pack, any two cards that total 9. Cover any single nines. Cover 10, jack, queen, king whenever two of these of the same suit are exposed. Continue covering the designated cards until there are no cards that can be covered (in which case the game is lost), or until the entire deck is dealt out. Then pick up the piles that would normally be covered—pairs where the top cards total 9, a pile with 9 as the top card, two piles with any same suit 10, J, Q, or K. If there are no remaining piles, the game is won.

Learning Skills

• addition

Ages: 5 to adult

In Turkey this is a fortune-telling game. You make a wish before you start. If you win the game it is considered a sign that your wish might come true.

Layout
Deal out the entire deck in thirteen piles of four face-down cards. Turn up the top card on each pile.

Object of the Game
To get rid of all the cards by removing them in pairs.

Play
Remove cards in pairs (cards of the same denomination), turning up the card that is uncovered with each removal. Continue until all cards are removed or no move is possible.

Learning Skills
• number recognition • matching

Ages: 6 to adult

My favorite solitaire as a child was Threes in the Corner. Even young children enjoy it, since it helps them practice moving up and down the number line. I've only recently discovered Quadrille. It calls on similar skills, but it is much prettier and somehow reminds me of *Alice in Wonderland.*

Layout

Arrange four queens in the center as a cross, with the Queen of Spades at the north, Queen of Clubs at the south, Queen of Hearts to the east, and Queen of Diamonds to the west.

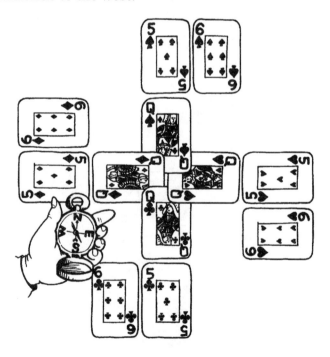

This is only to create a pleasing tableau, but learning and arranging this format will help the player's sense of direction and map-reading ability.

Around the queens arrange the fives and sixes, with the Five of Spades to the north of the Queen of Spades, the Six of Spades to the northeast; the Five of Hearts to the east of the Queen of Hearts, the Six of Hearts to the southeast; the Five of Clubs to the south of the Queen of Clubs, the Six of Clubs to the southwest; the Five of Diamonds to the west of the Queen of Diamonds and the Six of Diamonds to the northwest.

Object of the Game

The object of the game Quadrille is to build upward in suit on the sixes to the jacks; to build downward in suit on the fives to kings (5—4—3—2—A—K).

Play

Turn up cards from the deck one at a time, placing them on the appropriate "builds" where possible or turning them faceup on a trash (discard) pile.

When all the cards have been dealt out, they may be dealt a second time. As many as three "redeals" are permissible.

Learning Skills

• numerical ordering • learning the cardinal directions, north, south, east, and west

Old Card Riddle

♣ Why was the Shah of Persia the best Whist player in England? Because the farmers throw down their spades, the gentlemen give up their clubs, and ladies lose their hearts when they see the Shah's diamonds.

Ages: 8 to adult

Object of the Game

The object of Royal Square is to remove all four middle cards in a sixteen-card layout, leaving all face cards in a prescribed layout forming a square.

Layout

Sixteen cards are dealt out faceup to form a four-by-four matrix.

Lay them out like this: First, put down the center four cards—that is, the second and third cards of the second and third rows. However, if a face card turns up, place it on the outside border of the matrix according to the following arrangement. Kings go in the corners (at the beginning and end of the first and fourth rows). Queens go at the beginning and end of the second and third rows. Jacks are placed in the second and third slots of the first and fourth rows.

Then lay out the cards to fill in the remaining slots.

Play

When sixteen cards are laid out, cards may be removed from the layout in pairs that total 10 (6 + 4; 9 + A; 5 + 5; 7 + 3; 8 + 2) or a 10 may be removed by itself.

When all possible plays have been made, the empty slots needed to complete the matrix are filled from the deck. Play resumes, removing cards as before. Each time you deal cards to the layout, fill in the four center slots first, placing face cards in the outside slots as they turn up. If a face card cannot be placed in one of its designated slots because all are already filled, then the game is lost.

You win the game when all face cards are in their correct slot, and cards have all been removed from the middle.

Strategies

Before placing number cards on the perimeter, consider carefully what slot you are filling. Always try to leave at least one slot for each kind of face card that may turn up, remembering that if the face card can't be placed the game is lost.

Learning Skills

• addition • number facts under 10

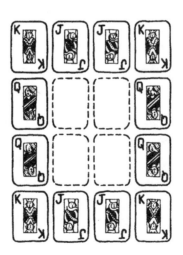

Here is what the winning game looks like.

GAMES

This chapter includes a variety of games, from the simple to the complex, for two or more players. These games are not just for children; many adults enjoy them, too. In fact, many games found here are direct steals from the standard adult repertoire. We've also added games that will appeal to the smallest child.

Ages: 6 to adult
Players: 2 or two teams of 2

This game is well known to Italian children. *Scopa* means "broom."

Object of the Game

The object of Scopa is to get the most points. The first player to get cards totaling 11 is the winner.

Equipment

An Italian deck of cards. If you don't have Italian cards, remove eights, nines, and tens from an ordinary deck of 52.

Point Value of Cards

All number cards equal their face value.
Jack = 8 points
Queen = 9 points
King = 10 points

First of All

The dealer deals four cards to each player and four faceup cards on the table.

Play

Players take turns playing a card from their hand. A card may be used as a "match" to take in a card of the same denomination. Or it can take in more than one card if the card to be played equals the total of two or more cards on the table.

For example, a 6 and a 2 on the table may be taken by a jack, a 3 and ace by a 4. When players take in cards, they keep them facedown in a pile in front of them.

If a player manages, at any point, to pick up the last card on the table, that is a "scopa." That card is turned up in the pile of accumulated cards, to be scored separately when the players tally their points.

After the four cards have been played out, the dealer deals four more to each player. The play continues until all cards have been dealt out. Then players tally their points.

Each Turned-Up Card (scopa) = 1 point
Each Seven = 1 point
King of Diamonds = 1 point
The Most Cards = 1 point
The Most Diamonds = 1 point

Learning Skills
• matching • addition • keeping track of several variables

♠ Some card decks feature useful tips, like cards with first-aid instruction or outdoor survival hints for campers in the wild.

KNUCKLES

Ages: 6 to 12
Players: 2

Sara, eleven, taught me this game. She said that a player could rap the table with her knuckles at any time during the game if she thought she had the lower score. Both players show their hands; the one with the lower score wins.

Object of the Game

The object of Knuckles is to end up with the cards totaling the lowest possible value.

Equipment

A deck of cards.

Point Value of Cards

Cards 2 to 10 are equal to their face value.
Ace = 1 point
Jack = 0 points
Queen and King = 10 points each

First of All

The dealer deals a hand of five cards to each player and places the rest of the deck facedown in the middle.

Play

The first player takes the top card of the pack, and he may exchange it for any card in his hand. He does this exchange only if the new card is lower than one of the cards in his hand. The discarded card is placed face-up beside the facedown pack. The next player may take the faceup card or pick the top card of the pack and either change it for a card in his hand or discard it. Play continues, with players changing cards in their hands for lower ones, until all the cards in the pack have been picked. The player with the lowest cards is the winner. The winner is, invariably, the one with the most jacks and aces.

Learning Skills
• concepts of "higher" and "lower" • addition

It has been said that the four suit symbols originally represented the four classes of society in medieval Europe. Spades represented the nobles, hearts the clergy, diamonds the merchants, and clubs the peasants and serfs. This ranking (spades, hearts, diamonds, and clubs), from the highest to the lowest, still holds in the popular card game Bridge.

BICHOS

Ages: 5 to 12
Players: 3 to 10

This game is popular with children in Portugal; the word *bichos* means "animals." In Spanish, *bicho* has multiple meanings—"animal," "insect," or "simpleton"—so beware.

Object of the Game

The object of the game Bichos is to be the first to get rid of all your cards.

Equipment

One, two, or three decks of cards, depending on the number of players. Use one deck for three or four; two decks for five or six; and three decks for larger groups.

First of All

Shuffle the decks together and deal out all cards in facedown stacks in front of the players. Each player chooses the name of an animal and announces it. Other players must remember each player's "animal" and use it in the game.

Play

All players simultaneously turn up the top card of their stack. If a player's card matches, in denomination, any other player's card, he calls out that player's "animal." The last player to call the animal correctly must take in the matching cards and add them to his stack.

If there are no matches, the cards remain faceup in front of the players and new cards are played on the faceup pile. At the next match, the loser takes in all the cards in the faceup pile. If there are three-way matches, and one player correctly calls out the animal names of the two players before his is called out, then the losers divide up the winner's cards. Play continues until one player has no cards left and is the winner.

Tips for Good Play

Portuguese children usually try to choose animal names that their opponents will find hard to remember—not just dog, cat, and horse, but names like orangutan, rhinoceros, okapi, and chinchilla.

Variation

Choose names from other semantic domains, e.g. vegetables, furniture, diseases. Switch categories from time to time during play to keep players on their toes.

Of course, if you wanted to test your memory of scientific names of animals or plants, these could also substitute.

Learning Skills

• visual scanning • fast visual responses • practice in visual discrimination • rapid word retrieval

Ages: 5 to adult
Players: 2 to 4

Object of the Game

The object of the game Finders Keepers is that players take in cards that total a predetermined sum.

Equipment

A deck of cards.

Point Value of Cards

Ace = 1 point
Two through ten equal their face value.
Jack = 11 points
Queen = 12 points
King = 13 points

For younger children, I sometimes let all face cards equal 10 points.

First of All

Lay out all the cards facedown in 6 rows of 8, with a 7th row of 4 cards.

Play

The first player names a number and then turns up any two cards. If the cards total that number, he takes in both cards. If not, he leaves one card faceup and turns the other over again in its original place.

The next player then turns up two cards and sees if he can make the predetermined sum with two or more of the faceup cards. If he is successful, he takes in the cards. If not, he leaves one faceup and turns over the other(s).

When a player succeeds in making the total, he chooses the next number that will be the sum the players try to make.

The winner is the player who has the most cards when all the cards are turned up.

Tips for Good Play

Try to remember the value and location of some of the cards that have been turned over and replaced. Knowing where a particular number is located allows a player to go directly to the card needed to complete a total.

After your turn, think carefully about which card you will leave faceup. You may be able to make it harder for the next player to get the cards that will equal the total he is after.

Learning Skills

• addition • visual–spatial concepts

At one time, playing cards were taxed, and you can find tax stamps on the packages of some old decks.

MARRIAGE

Ages: 4 to 12
Players: 3

Benoit, a teenage summer visitor from France, taught us his country's version of a familiar North American game. The French word and game title is *mariage,* which means "wedding." We've simply called it Marriage.

Object of the Game

The object of the game Marriage is to avoid holding the key card at the end.

Equipment

A deck of cards.

First of All

The dealer chooses the key card and removes the same color card of that denomination from the deck. Other players do not know which card has been chosen. The entire deck is dealt out.

Play

Players remove from the hand pairs of cards of the same color and denomination—for example, the Four of Hearts and the Four of Diamonds.

When all pairs have been removed, each player in turn may pick a card from the hand of the player to his right. As the same color pairs are formed, they are removed from the hand. The player left with the key card is the loser. ("*Pas de mariage,*" said Benoit, which means "no wedding.")

Learning Skills

• matching (color and number)

Ages: 5 to 14
Players: 2 to 4

With three or four players this game has more suspense and excitement, because you are never sure who is going to win the pile. This particular version comes from the British island of Barbados.

Object of the Game

The object of Suck the Well is to win all the cards by turning up high cards.

Equipment

A deck of cards.

First of All

For authentic Caribbean play, deal counterclockwise, from right to left. Deal the whole deck of cards out equally among all the players. Players keep their cards in a facedown pile in front of them.

Play

The player to the dealer's right begins, and play continues to the right. Cards are faced up by each player in turn, one at a time, on a pile in the center. The player who plays a "royal"—a face card or an ace—is eligible to take in the pile. But first, the player next in line must "pay" him by playing cards on his.

On a Jack—one card
On a Queen—two cards
On a King—three cards
On an Ace—four cards

However, if, while "paying," the player turns up a "royal," then payment stops and the next player must begin payment according to the above values. If none of the payment cards is a royal, then the player who played the last royal takes in all the cards in the pile, putting them on the bottom of his own stack. The player who took in the cards plays the next card. If a player has no more cards, he drops out of the game and play continues among remaining players. The player to get all the cards is the winner.

Learning Skills

• counting • distinguishing among face cards and responding appropriately

♥ In Devonshire, England, you'll find an inn called the Pack o' Cards Inn. It was built in the 17th century to celebrate the owner's luck at gambling. The inn has four floors, 52 windows, and 13 doors.

Ages: 6 to adult
Players: 2

Speed is a logical name for this frenzied race between two players to get their cards on the table.

Equipment

A deck of cards.

First of All

Deal two facedown piles of four cards each, one to the right of each player. These are the starter cards. Deal out the rest of the deck so that each player has a facedown pack. Players take the top four cards of their facedown piles as a hand, replacing cards as they are played so that they always hold a four-card hand.

Play

Players simultaneously turn up the top card of the starter cards to their right, placing the cards faceup in the middle of the table so that there are two cards side by side. These are the cards to be played on.

Players now, as fast as they can (with no regard for taking turns), try to play cards from their hands on the faceup piles. A card may be played, regardless of suit, if it is one more or one less than the card on top of the pile. Thus, on a 7 a player may play a 6 or an 8. On a king, a player may play a queen or an ace. As plays are made, players may take cards from their facedown stack, always keeping four cards in their hands.

When no more plays can be made, players, again

simultaneously, turn up the top card from the piles on their right onto the faceup playing piles, and play resumes. When the four-card stack is used up, turn over the faceup stacks to replace the stacks at the right. These are used to provide the starter cards. Play continues until one player gets rid of all his cards and is the winner.

Learning Skills
• visual scanning • fast visual–motor responses • moving up and down the number line

♠ There are many unsubstantiated theories about the origins of playing cards in China or India, but no real proof. There is, however, documented evidence that playing cards were used in Europe in 1377. A treatise in Latin, written by a German monk, describes the game of cards. Along with describing the game, he suggests that in it "there is a moral action of the virtues and vices." Also, the monk declares that card playing "is of service for mental relief and rest to the tired." "It is useful for idle persons and may be a comfort to them."

SWITCH

Ages: 5 to 12
Players: 2 to 6

There seems to be some version of Crazy Eights everywhere in the world. This version is played in Brisbane, Australia.

Object of the Game

The object of the game Switch is to be the first to get rid of all your cards.

Equipment

A deck of cards.

Point Value of Cards

Cards equal face value; face cards count 10 points each.

First of All

Deal eight cards to each player. Place the rest of the deck facedown in the middle. Turn up the top card of the deck and place it beside the deck.

Play

The players in turn must play a card to the turned-up pile. It may be a card of the same suit or denomination as the top card. However, if an ace is played, play is switched to any suit the player names.

Shuffle and deal the cards again until one player's score reaches a predetermined number, like 100 points, and that player is the loser. The first player to get rid of all the cards is the winner of the hand. Cards left in the losers' hands are added up and count against them.

Learning Skills

• set-changing • matching • classification • addition

Hundreds of decks of cards—novelty decks, decks from around the world, reproductions of antique playing cards, historical decks, and Tarot and other fortune-telling decks—are available. And you'll find them as you travel around the world. There are also many books on playing cards.

Ages: 6 to adult
Players: 3 to 6

There are more rules to remember in this game than Crazy Eights, yet all children seem to be able to retain the complex inventory of card values and procedures. This game promotes lots of arithmetic practice.

Object of the Game

The object of the game Creights (rhymes with *greats*) is to get rid of all your cards by playing a card that matches (according to a set of rules) the card that is faceup in the center of the table.

Equipment

For three or four players, use one deck of 52 cards; for more, use two decks shuffled together.

First of All

There are fifteen hands to a game. The number of cards dealt to each player changes with each hand, as follows:

Hand 1	8 cards	*Hand 9*	2 cards
Hand 2	7 cards	*Hand 10*	3 cards
Hand 3	6 cards	*Hand 11*	4 cards
Hand 4	5 cards	*Hand 12*	5 cards
Hand 5	4 cards	*Hand 13*	6 cards
Hand 6	3 cards	*Hand 14*	7 cards
Hand 7	2 cards	*Hand 15*	8 cards
Hand 8	1 card		

After the cards have been dealt, the remainder of the deck is placed facedown in the center of the table. The top card is turned up beside it.

Wild cards are eights and nines.

Play

Players, at their turn, must play a card from their hands faceup on top of the faceup pile. As in Crazy Eights, it must match the faceup card in suit or in denomination, or it may be a wild card. For example, if the faceup card is the Three of Clubs, the player may play any club, any 3, or any 8 or 9. If a player cannot make a play, he must take a card from the top of the deck. Play then passes to his left.

The card on top of the faceup pile may change the order of play according to the following rules. Play continues as usual unless a 4, 5, 6, 7, 8, 9, or 10 appears.

4 Skip one player.
5 All players take a card.
6 The player who plays a six must go again, and he

must play a card matching in suit or denomination or a wild card.

7 The player second from the left of the player who played the seven must draw a facedown card. Otherwise, play continues normally.

8 The player who plays an eight can name the suit the next player must match.

9 The player who plays a nine must name a suit different in color from the nine just played. That becomes the suit for the next player to match.

10 Play changes direction, so that the next play is made by the player to the right. Play continues counterclockwise until the next ten is played.

Special Rules for Twos and Aces

When a 2 is played, each player who follows must play either an ace or a 2. A wild card is not permissible. When the first 2 is played, a count begins. Players count 1 for each ace, 2 for each 2. If a player is unable to play an ace or a 2, he must add to his hand as many cards from the deck as the number of the count. Play passes to the next player, who plays normally—either a card of the same suit or denomination as the last card played, or a wild card. When the next 2 is played, the count begins again.

Play continues until one player "goes out"—gets rid of all his cards. If the facedown deck is used up before this happens, the player whose turn it is to draw shuffles the faceup pile—leaving the faceup card that determines his play—and places it facedown. Players are penalized for each shuffle that takes place at their turn.

Going Out

On the turn before a player "goes out," he must announce to the other players that he has only one card left. If he fails to notify his opponents, then he is not allowed to go out, but instead must draw two cards from the deck.

When a player does go out, the round does not end until the other players have responded to the card played. If the card played is a 6, the player must go again and therefore must draw cards. If he is not able to play the first card he draws, he will not be able to go out. Similarly, if his last card is a 2, the players are obliged to begin counting and playing twos or aces in turn. If his turn comes around while the count is still taking place, then he has to draw the requisite number of cards and will be unable to go out.

Scoring

After a player goes out, players add up the points in the cards they are left with according to these rules. Each three changes the scoring value of one other card in the hand to 3 points. Only eights are exempt. Here are the other point values.

Ace = 1 point
2 = 20 points
4 = 15 points
5 = 30 points
6 = 30 points
7 = 25 points

8 = 50 points
9 = 50 points
10 = 25 points
Jack = 10 points
Queen = 10 points
King = 10 points

Shuffling Penalty

For a player's first shuffle of the game, the penalty is 5 points. For each subsequent shuffle of the game (even in a new hand), the penalty is doubled—10 points for the second, 20 points for the third, etc.

The winner is the player with the lowest score at the end of 15 rounds.

Learning Skills

• mental flexibility • memory skills • right and left discrimination • matching • classification • computation

◆ Card decks that can be used by people with up to 95 percent visual impairment are available. The numbers on them are twice the size of the numbers on conventional playing cards, and two additional colors—blue and green—are used to help players who are unable to distinguish the suit markings.

Ages: 6 to adult
Players: 2 or two teams of 2

This game that Greek children play has echoes of Casino, the game I played most as a young child.

Equipment

Deck of 52 cards.

Object of the Game

To earn points by taking in key cards.

Value of Cards

Cards are not ranked in play, but jacks are wild and can be used as a match for any card. Cards taken in have the following point value.

Jack, Queen, King, Ace = 1 point each
Ten of Diamonds = 2 points
Two of Clubs = 2 points
Each Xeri = 10 points

First of All

Deal six cards to each player and four overlapping faceup cards on the table.

Play

The nondealer goes first. Players take turns playing a card from their hand to the top of the faceup cards. If the player has a card in hand of the same denomination as the card on the top or has a jack, then the player takes in that card. Cards taken in are kept in a facedown stack in front of the player.

When there is only one card left on the table and a player takes it in, it is turned faceup in the player's stack as a "xeri." Each "xeri" counts as 10 points when points are totaled.

After the six cards have been played, six more are dealt. Play continues until all cards are dealt and played. Then players' scores are totaled.

The game continues with dealers alternating until one player has 100 points and is the winner.

Learning Skills

• matching • addition • remembering key cards

♠ Cards were used educationally back in the 16th century. Decks were especially developed to teach philosophy, heraldry, geography, history, grammar, arithmetic, and spelling.

SPOOF

Ages: 5 to adult
Players: 2 or more

This game is also known as Drop 7, but I remember it as Fan-Tan, which I played as a child in Nova Scotia. In this version, the order of the suits is prescribed.

Object of the Game

To get rid of all the cards.

Equipment

A deck of cards.

First of All

All of the cards are dealt out.

Play

Each player is allowed to play one card. Player to dealer's right goes first, then each player in turn. To begin the play, the player must have the Seven of Diamonds. The player must pass if he cannot put down that card. The first player to have it places it on the table.

Players, in turn, may play the Seven of Clubs or the diamond card that follows or precedes the 7, placing the 6 on one side of the 7 and the 8 on the other side. Subsequent players may continue to place cards in sequence, building either up (on the 8) or down (on the 6), or they may play a 7. The Seven of Hearts may be played only after the Seven of Clubs has been played, and the Seven of Spades only after the Seven of Hearts. Players *must* play a card if they have a play.

Otherwise, they pass. Play continues until one player gets rid of all his cards and is the winner.

Strategies

If you have a choice of plays, choose the one most likely to prevent your opponent from going out. For example, if you suspect he has the Ace of Hearts and you have the two, you will hold it back so that he is unable to play that card.

Learning Skills

• remembering order of suits to be played (diamonds, clubs, hearts, spades) • numerical ordering (forward and backwards)

Last night I held a hand in mine,
So fair and pink and kind,
I swear I never held before
A fairer hand in mine.
I pressed it to my burning lips,
Kissed all five pink white parts
Of that dear hand I held last night—
The Royal Flush of Hearts.

KING'S MARKET

Ages: 5 to adult
Players: 2 to 8

Object of the Game

The object of King's Market is to play the key queen, which allows you to take the chip or token on the designated king, and be the first to get rid of your cards.

Equipment

A deck of cards and chips or tokens. You can use pennies or bottle caps for chips or tokens.

First of All

Put four kings in the middle. Players choose one of the kings to be the key card. Each player puts a chip on that king and one chip in the middle.

Deal out the whole pack, creating one extra hand. The dealer, if he doesn't like his own hand, can change it for the spare hand. If he does not want the spare hand, the next player may buy it, paying the dealer one chip.

Play

Whoever has the Ace of Spades plays first and plays that card. Or if there is no Ace of Spades, then the player who has the lowest spade plays it. The player who has the next card in that suit plays. If no one can play—because the next card is not available—the player who played the last card must play the lowest red card in his hand.

Players follow suit in sequence until that suit is stopped. The next player to play a card must play her

♠ 48 ♥

lowest black card. The player who plays the queen of the same suit as the king with the chip on it takes the chips.

The player to get rid of all his cards first is the winner and takes all the chips in the middle. If the chip on the king is not claimed, then it stays for the next turn.

Learning Skills

• concepts of lowest and highest • numerical ordering

◆ Japanese cards are unusually beautiful. They consist of 48 cards, each depicting a flower. The flowers are grouped in sets of four, each set representing a month. The cards are usually very small, with stenciled or enameled designs and black, glazed cardboard backs.

KING'S CORNER

Ages: 6 to Adult
Players: 2

I first played this game on a Caribbean island. I learned it from a 10 year old. It is undoubtedly a children's game, but I enjoyed playing it so much that I have indicated its suitability for a wide age range. I find it has much of the appeal of a solitaire. Players have to stay alert and scan the layout for possible plays.

Object of the Game

The object of King's Corner is to get rid of cards in the hand by playing them on the layout.

First of All

Remove the four kings from the deck and lay them faceup to form four diagonal corners for a layout that will have four more faceup cards.

Deal four faceup cards, placing each between two kings, to form the layout. Deal eight cards to each player. The deck is placed facedown in the middle.

Play

Players take turns. At each turn, a player draws a card from the top of the deck and may play cards onto the layout. A card may be played if it is opposite in color and one lower in value than a top faceup card. Thus, a red nine is played on a black ten, a black queen on a red king, etc. During a turn a player may make all possible plays. If any of the cards in the layout itself can

♠ 50 ♥

be placed on another one, the player may do so, filling the empty space with a card from his hand. Play continues until one player has no more cards and is the winner.

Learning Skills
• numerical ordering • principle of alternation
• visual scanning

Fifty-Two Pick Up

♣ Warning to all adults: If a child suggests you play this game, refuse politely.

This is not a real game but a time-honored part of the popular culture of childhood. It seems to be passed on by children to children, usually slightly younger—almost as part of an initiation into the world of card playing. One child says to the other, "Do you want to play Fifty-Two Pick Up?" The unsuspecting victim indicates his willingness. Then the initiator takes a deck of cards, throws them in the air, points to the cards scattered on the floor, and says, "Fifty-two pick up!"

Having been fooled, the child can hardly wait to find his own victim.

ODDS AND EVENS

Ages: 6 to 12
Players: 2

This game was created by a colleague of mine, Sylvia Riddell, as an imaginative approach to understanding the concept of odd and even numbers.

Object of the Game

To win all the cards.

Equipment

One deck of cards.

Point Value of Cards

Ace through 10 = face value   Queen = 12 points
Jack = 11 points   King = 13 points

First of All

One player picks a card. If it is an odd number, he is designated "Odd" and his opponent "Even." If it is an even number, the situation is reversed. Deal out all the cards so that each player has half the deck in a facedown pile.

Play

Players simultaneously turn up the top card of their packs. They add the numerical values of the two cards. If the total is odd, "Odd" takes it in and vice versa. Cards taken in are placed at the bottom of the player's pack. Play continues until one player wins all the cards.

Learning Skills

• addition • understanding the concept of odd and even numbers (not divisible by 2 and divisible by 2)

Ages: 6 to adult
Players: 2

After a summer of French immersion in Trois Rivières, my daughter brought back this game—as well as language facility. The game must have originated in Quebec; it is the only truly Canadian card game I know.

Object of the Game

The object of Hockey is to win the most goals in three periods. A period consists of all the hands played in one deck.

First of All

The dealer decides the number of cards he will deal in each hand and deals the same number to himself and to his opponent.

Play

The first player plays a card faceup to the center of the table. The next player partially covers it with a faceup card from his hand. If the card is of the same denomination (say, a 2 on a 2), it constitutes a pass. Two passes on two consecutive turns constitute a goal. So, for example, if player A plays a 3 and player B follows with a 3, that constitutes a pass. If player A then plays another 3, he scores a goal. However, if player B plays the fourth card of the denomination, the goal is nullified—and becomes no goal.

A jack is an automatic pass. If a player plays a jack on an immediately previous jack, he scores a goal. This can, of course, be canceled by a third jack. But the fourth jack played on that one will call back the goal.

When the cards are played out, the dealer deals another hand from the remaining cards and the play continues. Hands are dealt out until the deck is finished. This marks the end of the first period.

The deal changes hands for the second period, and then changes back for the third. If the score is tied at the end of three periods, the game goes into sudden-death overtime; the first player to score wins.

Learning Skills

• matching • the vocabulary of hockey

♠ Cards may be classified into standard and nonstandard playing cards. Standard cards are produced for conventional card games and contain little to distract the player. They usually have the appropriate suit markings of the country of origin, and they represent court cards in a fairly similar way.

Nonstandard cards, however, are products of an artist's imagination, and they may be humorous, educational, or artistic. Some of these cards are used for advertising or fortune-telling, while others serve as souvenirs of particular places, events, or expressions.

Ages: 5 to 12
Players: 2 to 4

Object of the Game

To be first to get rid of your cards.

First of All

Deal seven cards to each player. Put the remainder of the deck facedown in the middle. Turn up the top card of the deck and leave it faceup beside the deck. This card determines the first suit to be played.

Play

Player to the dealer's left must play a card of the turned-up suit. If he doesn't have it he keeps drawing cards from the deck until he can play one of that suit. The next player follows suit. (If he can't, he turns up cards until he gets a playable one.) The one who plays the highest card is considered the winner of the trick. The winner takes in the cards and puts them aside, then "leads" to the next play. The player who leads can play a card of any suit and other players must follow suit. If they cannot, they keep drawing cards until they can. Play continues as above.

When the deck is exhausted, play continues from the hand. If a player plays a suit and no one has cards to follow suit, he plays all the cards of that suit in his hand, and then plays a card of another suit. The first player to get rid of all his cards is the winner. Play can then continue among remaining players. The last one with cards in his hand is the Donkey. The number of cards in his hand tells what age donkey he is. For example, two cards signify a two-year-old donkey.

Learning Skills

• classification • relational value of numbers (higher, lower, highest, etc.)

♣ Consider cards in the arts. Several movies have been made about card games: *The Cincinnati Kid*, about poker; *A Big Hand for the Little Lady*, about poker; and *The Flamingo Kid*, about gin rummy. *Trick 13* is a novel, a murder mystery set in the world of international tournament bridge. *The Gin Game* was a successful Broadway play. The twentieth-century composer Gian Carlo Menotti wrote an opera called *The Game of Cards*.

In the collection of Her Majesty the Queen of Great Britain at Buckingham Palace is a painting by the Dutch painter Pieter de Hooch (1629–c. 1684) called *The Card Game*. Another painting, *Il Baro* by Michelangelo da Caravaggio (1573–1610) shows two young boys playing cards for money. A bystander, looking over the shoulder of one of them, is signaling to the other. The cards in the picture, with suit markings, but no numbers in the corner, look very much like my reproductions of Early American cards.

GO TO PACK

Ages: 5 to 12
Players: 2 or more

This game is a version of Donkey, and both games are played in the islands of the Caribbean.

Object of the Game

To be the first to get rid of your cards.

First of All

Players decide on the penalty for each card remaining in the loser's hand. The children from Barbados with whom I played used penalties, such as the number of times to do the dishes or the number of verses to sing.

Deal three or four cards to each player. Put the pack (deck) facedown in the middle. Turn up the top card and place it beside the pack. This determines the suit to be played.

Play

The first player must play a card following the suit of the turned-up card. If he can't play a card of that suit, he "goes to pack," picking up cards one at a time until he can play. Other players do the same. The player who played the highest card takes in the pile and makes the next play. The card he plays determines the suit of the next round. The play continues in this way until there are no more cards in the pack.

When there are no more cards in the pack and the player cannot follow suit, he picks up the card and one of his opponents must give him a card to play.

The first player to get rid of all his cards is the win-

ner. Each card remaining in the loser's hand determines how many penalties he pays. With four cards
left over, he may have to read four comics aloud.

Tips for Good Play

Try to play high cards in order to be the one to decide
what suit is played.

   Try to keep track of suits that have been played and
of how many cards in that suit have been played. This
will give you an idea of what suits remain in an opponent's hand.

Learning Skills

• classification • relational value of numbers (higher,
lower, highest, etc.)

 The number of possible thirteen-card
bridge hands is 635,013,559,600.

Ages: 6 to adult
Players: 4 to 6

Object of the Game

The object of the game is to take in tricks so that you can add to your hand from the stack and to be the only player in the game with cards remaining.

Equipment

A deck of cards; chips or tokens.

Value of Cards

From lowest to highest, 2 through 10, then jack, queen, king, and ace. Aces are the highest cards.

First of All

"Cut the cards" to determine what suit will be trump. If the cut cards reveal a Four of Diamonds, for instance, then diamonds becomes "trump," which means that if a player cannot present a card to match a particular suit, he may play any diamond (a trump card) to win the play.

Each player puts a chip in the pot. Deal four cards each to four players; five cards each to five players; six cards each to six players. Place deck in the center of the table.

Play

The player to the dealer's left leads. The players follow suit in turn if they can. If a player cannot follow suit, he may play a trump or any card from another suit. If no trump card has been played, the highest card of the suit led takes in the trick. Otherwise, the player with the highest trump card takes in the trick. The winner of the trick then picks the top card of the deck which leads to the next trick. Play continues. When a player has no more cards, he withdraws from the game. The last player left holding cards is the winner and takes in the pot.

Before each new hand the deck is shuffled, cards are cut to determine the trump card, and each player puts a chip in the pot.

Learning Skills

• classification (following suit) • number values

♠ The record for the youngest life master in bridge was set at a tournament in Montreal by Douglas Hsieh, age 11 years, 10 months. Douglas attributed his good intellectual ability to early card playing—particularly games of concentration—when he was just a preschooler.

Ages: 6 to adult
Players: 4

King, played by children in Portugal, is really six different games played in sequence. Each is a nice little game in its own right. When played as a mega-game, the rules change with each new hand. Players must continually change their set and remember the objectives of the current hand.

Object of the Game

To win or to avoid tricks, to win or to avoid key cards, depending on which hand in the sequence is being played.

The game consists of twelve hands. The first six hands are "positive," where players get credit for key cards. The next six hands are "negative," where players lose points for key cards.

First of All

Players draw cards to determine who is the dealer. They keep drawing until one player draws a king and becomes the dealer of the first hand. After that, deal passes to the right.

All of the cards are dealt out. The dealer, after looking at his cards, names the trump (the suit that will rank the highest for this hand) or decides that there will be no trump.

Play

The player to the dealer's right plays the first card. All players must follow suit if they can. The highest card takes in the trick. If a player cannot follow suit, a trump card may be played and a trump card outranks any other card. In the case of two trump cards, the higher trump wins the trick.

Rules for Individual Hands

POSITIVES   The object of the game is to take in cards or tricks.

Hand 1   As many tricks as possible. Score 25 for each trick taken.
Hand 2   Hearts. Each heart scores 20 points.
Hand 3   Women (queens). Score 50 points for each.
Hand 4   Men (kings and jacks). Score 30 points for each.
Hand 5   King of Hearts. Score 150 points.
Hand 6   Last two tricks. Score 100 points for the next-to-last trick and 150 points for the last trick.

NEGATIVES   The object of the game is to avoid tricks or cards.

Hand 7   Tricks. Lose 25 points for each trick taken.
Hand 8   Hearts. Lose 20 points for each heart taken.
Hand 9   Women. Lose 50 points for each queen taken.
Hand 10   Men. Lose 30 points for each king or jack taken.
Hand 11   King of Hearts. Lose 150 points if this card is taken.
Hand 12   Last two tricks. The player loses 100 points if the next-to-last trick is taken, and the player loses 150 points if the last trick is taken.

The winner is the player with the highest score at the end of twelve hands.

Learning Skills

• mental flexibility • memory skills • classification
• relational value of numbers (higher, lower, highest, etc.) • addition • subtraction

Ages: 8 to adult
Players: 3

Object of the Game

The game's objective is to make the designated number of tricks in each hand and to be the first to achieve a score of 0.

First of All

Each player picks a card to determine the number of tricks he must make. If two players pick cards of the same denomination, they pick again. The holder of the highest card must make nine tricks, the middle card five tricks, and the lowest card two tricks. The holder of the highest card is the dealer. Aces are the highest cards.

The entire deck is dealt to the three players, except for the last four cards, which are placed facedown at the side. The dealer, after inspecting his cards, may choose to discard four and take the four facedown cards.

Play

The player to the dealer's left plays any card. Other players must follow suit. The highest card takes in the trick and leads to the next trick. If a player cannot follow suit, he can play any card. Play continues until all cards have been played. Players count their tricks.

Scoring

Each player begins with a score of 9. The first person to get 0 is the winner. If a player makes his designated number of tricks, his score stays the same. For every trick over that designated number, he loses a point. For every trick under, he gains a point. (That means that for every player who goes up, someone else goes down proportionately.)

The penalty for making fewer than the assigned number of tricks: On the next deal, the player must give as many cards as points gained to the person who lost points. Each person receiving cards must give the penalized player the highest card in her hand. On the next deal (and all subsequent deals), the designated number of tricks for each player changes: 9 becomes 2, 5 becomes 9, and 2 becomes 5.

The game continues until one player reaches 0 and is the winner.

Learning Skills

• classification • number values • subtraction

♥ A postage stamp with the Queen of Hearts on it was issued by Bermuda in January 1975 to mark a world bridge championship.

Ages: 7 to adult
Players: 2 to 4

This game from France is one of innumerable versions of rummy. In this version, the wild card changes from hand to hand. *Frimé* means "showing off."

Object of the Game

The objective is to be first to get rid of all your cards.

Equipment

A deck of cards.

First of All

Deal seven cards to each player. Then place the deck in the center of the table and turn up the top card and place it beside the deck.

Play

The player to the dealer's left takes a card (the turned-up card if he wants it; otherwise the top card of the pack) and discards one. Play continues to the left. At a player's turn he may *meld* (lay down sets of cards face-up in front of him). Permissible melds are "three of a kind" (three or more cards of the same denomination) or runs of three or more cards of the same suit in sequence.

Players (at their turn) may add to layouts on the table. When the fourth member of a set has been added, the four cards are turned over. As soon as a player puts down all his cards, the other players count the point value of cards in their hands. Each player's cards count *against* him.

The winner is the player with the lowest score after a designated number of hands.

Point Value of Cards

Ace through 10 equal the card's face value. Ace counts as 1 point.

Jack, Queen, King = 10 points each

Wild card = 15 points

Aces are wild in the first hand, twos in the second, then threes, and so on.

Learning Skills

• classification • numerical ordering • memory skills • set-changing • addition

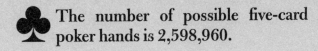 The number of possible five-card poker hands is 2,598,960.

GIMME

Ages: 7 to adult
Players: 5 or more

Object of the Game

The object of Gimme is to be first to get rid of all the cards in your hand. Each game consists of seven hands, each of which begins in the same way.

Equipment

Two decks of cards with jokers shuffled together. Use three decks for seven or more players.

First of All

Deal eleven cards to each player. The dealer puts the rest of the pack in the center of the table and turns the top card faceup. The player to the dealer's left may take that card. If he doesn't want it, any player who does may say "Gimme." The one closest to the dealer gets it, but he must take the top facedown card along with it.

Play

Each player in turn picks a card from the top of the deck and discards one in a separate discard pile face-up beside the deck. The player to his left may pick up the discard, but if he does not, other players may say "Gimme" and the game proceeds as above.

A player is allowed only three "Gimme's" in any hand. That is, he may obtain a maximum of seventeen cards. Players, at their turn, may *meld* cards—lay sets faceup in front of them—according to the rules below for the seven hands.

A *set* consists of three to five cards of the same denomination. A *run* consists of four to seven cards of the same suit in sequence.

First Hand	Two sets
Second Hand	One set, one run
Third Hand	Two runs
Fourth Hand	Three sets
Fifth Hand	Two sets, one run
Sixth Hand	Two runs, one set
Seventh Hand	Three runs

The sets for each hand do not have to be laid down at the same time, nor do the runs.

Jokers are wild and may substitute for any card in a run or set.

A player, at his turn, may also put down cards that complement opponents' melds. For example, if there is a set of sevens on the table, a player can meld a 7 from his own hand; if an opponent has a run of Two of Hearts—Three of Hearts—Four of Hearts—Five of Hearts, a player can meld an Ace of Hearts or a Six of Hearts from his hand. A player can do the same with his own hand.

A hand ends as soon as one player has no more cards. Other players total the value of all the cards left in their hands. These count against them. If, at any point in the game, one player has more than seventeen cards in his hands (that is, has taken more than three "Gimme's"), all of the cards in his hand count against him.

Point Value of Cards

Joker = 50 points
Ace = 25 points
Jack, Queen, King (all face cards) = 10 points each
All other cards = 5 points

The winner is the player with the lowest score after all seven hands have been played.

Learning Skills

• classification • numerical ordering • mental flexibility • memory skills • visual scanning • addition • counting by tens (the efficient way to score the face cards in your hand)

 There are 15,920,024,220 different hands possible in gin rummy.

BACK-ALLEY BRIDGE

Ages: 7 to adult
Players: 2 to 4

Also known as Open Rummy, this is my favorite rummy game. It is thoroughly involving and fast-moving. It keeps players on their toes, always engaged in planning strategic moves.

Equipment
Two decks of 52 cards shuffled together.

Object of the Game
The object of Back-Alley Bridge is to lay out sets and runs in order to be the first to get rid of all the cards.

Point Value of Cards
All cards, ace through ten, equal their face value.
Ace = 1 point
Face cards = 10 points each

However, in play, aces can be low or high, so permissible runs would include these possibilities.

Ace—2—3
Queen—King—Ace
King—Ace—2

First of All
Deal seven cards to each player and place the deck in the middle of the table.

Play
Each player, in turn, takes the top card off the deck and adds it to his hand. After picking a card, a player

may "meld"—lay down cards in sets or runs faceup in the center of the table. Permissible melds are three or more cards of the same denomination (but of different suits) or 3 same-suit cards in sequence (like Two—Three—Four of Spades). If a player cannot meld, play passes to the left.

At any turn a player may put down all possible melds, add to sets or runs on the table, and rearrange sets and runs on the table to allow further play. Sets and runs can be taken apart and reassembled, as long as the result yields runs or sets of at least three cards. For example, if, on the table, there is a set of Jack—Queen—King—Ace of Diamonds and Eight—Nine—

Ten—Jack of Spades and the player's hand contains a Jack of Hearts, the player may remove the Jack of Diamonds and Jack of Spades from their respective runs and lay them down with the Jack of Hearts to make a set of jacks.

Rearrangements may involve many different layouts in which cards are ingeniously recombined to allow a play. When all possible moves have been made, the player knocks on the table to indicate that the next player may proceed. Play continues until one player has no more cards and is the winner of the hand.

Other players count up the value of the cards remaining in their hands. Those points are credited to the score of the player who won the hand. At the end of an agreed number of hands, the player with the highest score is the winner of the game.

Learning Skills
• ordering • classification • planning • mental flexibility • problem-solving

♥ The total number of different sequences possible in a 52-card deck is a figure 68 digits long.

DRAT!

Ages: 7 to adult
Players: 2 to 4 or more

Here's another version of rummy; this one is from England.

Object of the Game

The object is to be first to get rid of all the cards in your hand.

Equipment

Two decks of cards with jokers. Wild cards are jokers and twos. If there are five or more players, use three decks.

First of All

Deal eleven cards to each player. Put the remainder of the deck in the center of the table and turn up the top card.

Special Rules

A game consists of twelve or more hands. There are twelve "contracts" to be made in turn. Each player must make contract number 1 before he can make number 2, even if other players are on a second or third hand.

Here are the twelve successive contracts.

Contract 1   Two sets of three. (A set is cards of the same denomination.)
Contract 2   One set of three; one run of four. (A run is cards of the same suit in sequence.)
Contract 3   Two sets of four.

Contract 4	Two runs of four.
Contract 5	One set of four; one run of four.
Contract 6	Three sets of three.
Contract 7	One set of three; one run of seven.
Contract 8	Two sets of three; one run of four.
Contract 9	Two sets of five.
Contract 10	Two runs of five.
Contract 11	One run of eight.
Contract 12	One run of ten.

In any given set or run, wild cards cannot exceed the number of natural cards used.

Aces may be high (follow a king in a run) or low (precede a two).

Play

The player to the dealer's left may pick up the turned-up card, or he may take the top card of the facedown pack. When he has taken a card, he discards one on the faceup pile. The next player may take either the top faceup card or the top facedown card. He then discards one. Play proceeds to the left. At a player's turn, he may meld cards in keeping with his contract. He does not have to meld the entire contract at once. For example, if he has to make two sets, he can lay down one at a time.

After a contract is made, the other cards in the hand can be placed on contracts already on the board. For example, a 2 may be placed on a set of twos, or a Ten of Spades on a run of Six—Seven—Eight—Nine of Spades.

When a player is out, other players' remaining cards count against them.

Point Value of Cards

Joker = 50 points
Deuce (2) = 50 points
Ace = 25 points
9 to King = 10 points
3 to 8 = 5 points

Scoring

When the first person goes out after the twelfth contract has been made, the winner is the player with the lowest score—even if that player has not completed Contract 12.

Variation

Another version of rummy is called Frustration. It is played out just like Drat!, except twelve cards are dealt to each player. In addition, there are ten contracts to be made, the only wild cards are jokers, and the scoring is different.

Here are the ten contracts for Frustration.

Contract 1   Two sets of three.
Contract 2   One set of three; one run of three.
Contract 3   One run of four; one set of four.
Contract 4   Two runs of four.
Contract 5   One run of four; two sets of three.
Contract 6   One run of five; one set of three.
Contract 7   One run of seven; one set of three.
Contract 8   Two runs of four; one set of three.
Contract 9   Four sets of three.
Contract 10 Two runs of five.

Penalty Points for Frustration

Here are the penalty points for cards left in the hand when the game is over.

Joker = 20 points
Ace = 15 points
10, Jack, Queen, King = 10 points each
2 through 9 = 5 points each

Learning Skills

• classification • numerical ordering • mental flexibility • memory skills • visual scanning • addition • counting by tens (the efficient way to score the face cards in your hand)

HIT THE MARK

Ages: 6 to 12
Players: 2 to 4

I've named this card game after an eight-year-old boy, Mark, who taught it to me.

Object of the Game

To accumulate low cards and to have the cards totaling the lowest value.

Point Value of Cards

Ace = 1 point
2 through 10 = face value
King and Queen = 10 points each
Jack = 0 points

First of All

Deal five facedown cards to each player.

Play

Players take turns facing up cards from the center pile. At his turn, each player may trade one of his facedown cards for a faceup card, immediately turning the new card facedown in its place. The discarded card is added to the faceup pile and may be taken by an opponent if he wants to make a trade.

At any point in the game, a player who thinks his cards have a low total value may "knock." By knocking on the table, he announces that he wants to place his cards faceup. All players then do so. The winner is the player whose cards have the lowest total value.

Tips for Good Play

Players choose low-value cards and try to remember their position in the facedown array. This is essential so that they don't inadvertently trade them later in the game.

Learning Skills

• visual memory for sequence • addition

Some of the baffling card tricks done by magicians are done with a "stripper" deck. This is a deck that is very slightly tapered so that one end of the deck is narrower than the other. The difference is hardly visible to the eye, but when a card is reversed in the deck, the magician's fingers can immediately detect it.

MARK'S PLACE

Ages: 7 to adult
Players: 4 to 5

One mathematical concept important to grasp is that of place value. Understanding it is basic to understanding regrouping and to reading and writing multi-digit numbers. Mark's Place is a fun way to learn this concept.

Object of the Game

To get the highest value four-digit number, with a spade in the thousands place (on the left), a heart in the hundreds place (second from the left), a diamond in the tens place (third from the left), and a club in the ones place (on the right).

Equipment

Use a forty-card deck (with face cards removed).

Value of Cards

Spades	Thousands (e.g., Five of Spades = 5,000)
Hearts	Hundreds (e.g., Two of Hearts = 200)
Diamonds	Tens (e.g., Seven of Diamonds = 70)
Clubs	Ones (e.g., Nine of Clubs = 9)

First of All

Deal four facedown cards to each player. Place the remainder of the deck in the center of the table and turn up the top card.

Play

The player to the dealer's left may take the turned-up card and exchange it for one of his cards, turning the card faceup that he does not want and placing it next to the deck to form a discard pile. If he does not want the faceup card, he takes the top card and can either exchange it for one of his cards or discard it. Play continues to the left, with each player having the option of taking the top faceup card on the discard pile or the top card of the pack.

As soon as a player thinks he has a card of each suit in the correct place and believes he has constructed the highest four-digit number of the group, then he can "knock." This is a demand that all players turn up their cards and compare them.

Scoring

If the player who knocked does have the highest value, he gets from each player the difference between his number and the highest value number that player can construct. If a player does not have the required suit in its place, then he considers that he has a zero in that place. For example, if a player's turned-up cards are Three of Hearts, Seven of Hearts, Two of Diamonds, and Six of Diamonds, then his number is 720; if he has Two of Spades, Five of Hearts, Four of Clubs, Eight of Clubs, then his number is 2,508.

If a player has a higher number than the player who knocked, he gets double the value of the differences between his number and the knocker's number and, from each of the other players, the difference between his number and theirs.

The first player whose score totals 10,000 is the winner.

Variation

In this variation, the object of the game is to get the lowest possible number. To qualify, players must have one card in each suit in the correct spot. Include jacks in the deck (Jack = 0). Needless to say, the Jack of Spades will be the most sought-after card.

Learning Skills

• an understanding of place value • the reading and constructing of multi-digit numbers • directional awareness • visual memory for position in a horizontal array • subtraction involving multi-digit numbers

Playing-card collectors note, among other things, the dimensions and shape of the card and how court cards are represented. They also note the card's corner indices, back, border, corner (whether rounded off or square), and edges (which may be metallic). They also consider the deck's packaging.

SEVEN AND A HALF

Ages: 7 to adult
Players: 2 to 6

During lectures on card games, I often learn more than I teach. One class of language specialists produced this game, offered by a Sicilian man as *Sette e Mezzo*. A Venezuelan woman recognized it as *Siete y Medio*. Both played it with a forty-card deck, called Italian cards by one and Spanish cards by the other.

Object of the Game

The object of the game Seven and a Half is to get cards totaling as close to 7½ as possible without exceeding it.

Equipment

One deck of Italian or Spanish cards, or an ordinary deck with eights, nines, and tens removed. Chips or counters.

Point Value of Cards

All numerical cards are worth their face value (ace = 1, 2 = 2, etc.). Face cards = ½.

First of All

One player is selected as dealer. Players begin with an equal number of chips. These are used to bet against the dealer (that is, to bet that one's own hand will be closer to 7½ than the dealer's). Players may agree on a maximum bet.

The dealer gives each player, including himself, one facedown card. Each player places a bet.

Play

Beginning at the dealer's left, each player, in turn, decides whether to "stand pat" (take no more cards) or ask for another card. If, on taking another card, the total of the cards is more than 7½, then that player's bet immediately goes to the dealer. When a player decides to "stand pat," the dealer moves on to the next player. When all the players have drawn cards or overdrawn, the dealer completes his own hand. Then all cards are faced up.

Settlement: If the dealer goes over 7½, he pays each player who has not gone over 7½ the amount of the player's bet. If the dealer has 7½ or less, then the players having the same number are tied and no chips change hands. Players having less than the dealer pay their bet to the dealer. Players closer to 7½ than the dealer win the amount of their bet from him.

Comments

A perfect hand is 7 and a face card. Players may want to stand pat at 5. Although most players will not draw more than two cards, a player who initially gets several face cards may draw several before there is a real danger of going over.

Learning Skills

- addition • understanding the fractional value of $\frac{1}{2}$
- adding halves • calculating probabilities

♠ The Casino in Caesars Hotel in Atlantic City, New Jersey, reportedly uses 500 decks of cards each day.

Ages: 6 to adult
Players: 2

Object of the Game

The object of the game Add and Subtract is to be the first to reach the desired total (70 for "add"; 30 for "subtract").

Value of Cards

All cards have face value.
Jack = 11 points
Queen = 12 points
King = 13 points

First of All

This is a game for two. Both players pick a card. The player with the higher card is "Add." The other is "Subtract." Deal out the entire deck so that each player has half the deck in a facedown pile in front of him.

Play

The play begins with 50. The two players take turns placing their top cards on a central pile and adding or subtracting the card's value from the cumulative total. Here is a sample of what might happen in play.

Player	Card Played	Player Says
Add	7	57 (50 + 7)
Subtract	9	48 (57 – 9)
Add	3	51 (48 + 3)
Subtract	King	38 (51 – 13)

Scoring

If the total reaches 70, the player designated Add is the winner. If it falls to 30, then Subtract is the winner. If the cards run out before there is a winner, reshuffle them and turn them over.

Variations

Here's one variation. Start at 0, so that players use negative numbers. If the total reaches +20, Add wins; if it goes down to −20, Subtract is the winner.

Here's a second possible variation. Black numbers are positive. Red numbers are negative. (You could consider it an introduction to the accountant's "in the red"!) Players add to or subtract from the cumulative total, depending on the card they turn up. If players start at 50, the first player to reach 75 or 25 is the winner.

Allow the use of a calculator for young players who don't know number facts by heart and who can't make rapid mental calculations.

Learning Skills

• mental addition and subtraction • variations offer practice in using a calculator and practice in adding and subtracting negative numbers

Ages: 6 to 12
Players: 2

Object of the Game

The object of Zero is to win all the cards.

Equipment

A deck of cards.

Point Value of Cards

Cards are equal to their face value.

Jack = 11 points
Queen = 12 points
King = 13 points
Ace = 1 point

Black cards have positive value (+).
Red cards have negative value (–).

First of All

Divide the deck between the two players.

Play

Both players play simultaneously, as in the game War. Each turns up two cards at the same time. The player whose total value is closest to zero (0) takes in all four cards and puts them in a facedown pile.

For example, if player A has the Four of Spades and Queen of Diamonds (+4 and –12 = –8) and player B has the Four of Diamonds and King of Clubs (–4 and +13 = +9), then player A is the winner. In the case of a tie (say, player A has +2 and player B has –2), then each player turns up two more cards and totals them. The winner of that trick takes in all eight cards.

Learning Skills

• adding and subtracting negative numbers

Playing cards were used for over 300 or 400 years without indices for denominations (A, K, Q, J, or numbers) and without suit symbols in the corners. Cards had to be read full front to figure out their suit and value.

Corner indices were introduced in the 19th century for poker players. New decks with these indices were called "squeezer decks" because the indices allowed players to squeeze cards in the hand together and still read the cards.

JACKBLACK

Ages: 7 to adult
Players: any number

This game allows you to subtract points, rather than adding them. Instead of trying to get cards totaling 21 as in Blackjack, players start with 21 and subtract card totals to get as close to 0 as possible.

Object of the Game

The object of Jackblack is to get cards totaling 0, or as close to 0 as possible, and to obtain a smaller total than the dealer without going below 0. The value of cards in a player's hand is subtracted from the original 21. Each player in the game plays and bets against the dealer.

Equipment

Deck of 52 cards; chips or tokens.

Point Value of Cards

Jack, Queen, and King each count as 10.
2 to 10 each counts as its own face value.
Ace counts as 1 or 11.

First of All

Deal cards faceup around to all the players. The first player receiving a jack becomes the dealer and banker. Thereafter, the deal passes to the player to his left.

Players begin with an equal number of chips or counters. These are used to bet against the dealer. That is, the player bets that his own hand will be closer to 0 than the dealer's. A maximum bet is decided on by all players in advance. Before the deal, all players except the dealer place their bets—1, 2, or 3 chips, for instance.

When the deal begins, each player has 21 points. The dealer gives each player, including himself, one card faceup and one facedown, one at a time, in rotation to the left.

Play

Each player checks his cards for Jackblack, which consists of an ace and a ten-point card (11 + 10). This gives a total of 0 (21 – 21). If the dealer has Jackblack, each player, unless he has Jackblack himself, must give the dealer twice the amount of his bet. If a player has Jackblack and the dealer does not, he collects twice his bet from the dealer. If a player and the dealer both have Jackblacks, the dealer wins.

If the dealer does not have Jackblack, and after all players' Jackblacks have been paid off, the other players may draw a card. Each player in turn may ask for cards in order to bring his total as close to zero as possible. He asks for one card at a time (saying "Hit me") until he is satisfied to "stand pat." Should he go below 0 (–1, –2, etc.), he immediately shows his cards and the dealer collects the bet. After all the players have drawn cards, the dealer then faces up both of his cards and draws if he wants to.

Settlement: If the dealer goes below 0, he pays each player who has not overdrawn the amount of his bet. When the dealer has 0 or more, and the player is tied, the dealer wins. Players having more than the dealer pay their bet to him. Players closer to 0 than the dealer win the amount of their bet from him.

Learning Skills

• subtraction • calculating probabilities (that a card of a particular value might turn up)

♥ Cards were played on the ships sailed by Christopher Columbus and Spanish explorers. They taught card games to the natives in Central America and North America. Native Americans made cards of animal hides and painted them in the Spanish style.

THREE-CARD INDIAN POKER

Ages: 7 to adult
Players: 3

Object of the Game

To guess correctly the relative position of your number: high, low, or in the middle.

Equipment

A deck of cards; chips or tokens.

First of All

Remove the face cards and tens. Deal each player three cards. After looking at them, players turn them over and mix them thoroughly so that they have no idea of the relative positions of the cards. Then, without looking at the faces, they each raise the three cards and hold them to their foreheads, creating a three-digit number, visible to their opponents.

Play

Each player, after consulting his opponents' exposed cards, bets, putting in 2 chips, on the position of his own three-digit number. Then all players look at their cards. The winner, the one who bet correctly, takes in all the chips. If two players bet correctly, they divide the pot. If all three are correct, or all three are wrong, the chips stay to enrich the next pot.

Tips for Good Play

The player (P), knowing the three digits in his number, though not what place each occupies, may be able to calculate the probabilities of his relative position. If

P's digits are, for example, 3, 7, and 8, and opponents' numbers are 452 and 921, P is twice as likely to be in the "middle" (with 7 or 8 in the 100's place) than "low" (with 3 in the 100's place). If P goes second or third, and other players have already made bets, P is in an even better position to make a guess that takes the opponents' reasoning into consideration.

Variation

Players do not see their own cards, but they are told the total of their three cards. With only that information and the view of each of the opponents' three-digit number, players each guess whether their number is highest, lowest, or in the middle.

Learning Skills

• practice in reading three-digit numbers • place value • calculating probabilities • deductive reasoning

MULTIPLICATION RUMMY

Ages: 8 to 16
Players: 2 to 4

Object of the Game

The object of Multiplication Rummy is to be first to lay down all your cards.

Equipment

One deck with face cards removed.

First of All

Players agree on what multiplication table they will be playing (such as the six-times multiplication table). As a variation, they may agree to play for four deals (complete run-throughs of the deck), starting with the six-times table and increasing it by one each deal. Deal seven cards to each player. Put the remaining deck in the middle and turn up the top card.

Play

The first player may take the exposed card or the top card of the deck. He must discard a card from his hand, placing it on top of the faceup card. Play continues in this fashion.

Players, at their turn, may lay down a card or combinations of two or three cards, using the numbers to form the digits of numbers that are multiples of the agreed-on number. If, for example, the game is built around the eight-times table, a player may lay down a 6 and a 4, as 64, because $8 \times 8 = 64$.

Tens may be used in two ways: a 10 can be laid out with another card placed across it to indicate that the

10 is being multiplied by that number. Thus, if we were playing "Eights" (which uses the eight-times multiplication table), a 10 could be played with a 4 across it to stand for 40 ($5 \times 8 = 40$).

Tens can also be used to represent the number 10. For example, in playing "Nines," a player might lay down a 10 and an 8 as 108, because $12 \times 9 = 108$.

Play continues until one player gets rid of all his cards and is the winner of that deal.

Scoring

To calculate their points, losers count the cards remaining in their hands and multiply the number by the key number for that deal. So, if they are playing "Eights," then the number is 8.

The overall winner is the player with the lowest number of points at the end of four deals.

Suggestion

For very young children who do not know their multiplication tables, have the tables available, or provide

the player who needs it with a calculator. The repetition provided by playing will help make these multiplication facts automatic.

Learning Skills

• speedy multiplication

The deck of cards is sometimes likened to an almanac. The 52 cards remind us that there are 52 weeks in a year; 12 face cards suggest the 12 months of the year. Four suits suggest the four seasons of the year. And if we add up all the spots in a deck of cards—one for an ace, two for a two, three for a three, and so on up to 11 for a jack, 12 for a queen, 13 for a king, and one more for a Joker—then we get the total of 365, the number of days in a year.

THREE-CARD BRAG

Ages: 6 to adult
Players: any number

Object of the Game

The object of Three-Card Brag is to have the highest hand.

Equipment

Deck of cards; chips or tokens.

Value of Cards

Card values, in descending order, are A, K, Q, J, 10 through 2.

Here are hand values in ascending order.

Pairs   Two cards of the same denomination
Three of a Kind   Three cards of the same denomination
Run   Three cards in ascending order, regardless of suit, like Two of Spades—Three of Hearts—Four of Diamonds
Flush   Any three cards of the same suit
Running Flush   Three cards in sequence of the same suit

If two players have the same kind of hand, the highest card values win.

First of All

Deal three facedown cards to each player. All players "ante"—put a chip in the pot to indicate they are in the game.

Play

Players in turn look at cards and either "fold" (go out of the game) or place a chip in the pot, indicating that they bet their hand is high. When all players have placed their bets, hands are turned over and the highest hand wins. If there are no pairs, runs, flushes, etc., then the hand with the highest card wins.

Learning Skills

• matching • ordering • classifying

Court cards with double figures that could be viewed from either end appeared in the 19th century. Since these cards could be recognized faster, they helped players to play games faster.

Ages: 8 to adult
Players: 2 to 6

This game, which originated in Texas, is played by serious gamblers at the Poker World Series in Las Vegas. Although adults generally associate poker and all its variants with the dissolute world of the casino, with fortunes and time squandered, poker is really a lovely game, which can help develop both intellectual and social skills. Kids can have a wonderful time playing it, and they can learn a lot in the process.

The Poker Bluff

Poker is a gambling game, and betting is essential to the play, so there have to be stakes. Chips or tokens should be used that can be exchanged for something of real value. In a family, it can be privileges; for example, ten red chips can be cashed in for the right not to make the bed that day; in a classroom, for a night with no homework.

In poker, actually known as *bluff* in French, bluffing is very much part of the action. Bluffing—pretending to have a good hand, thereby scaring other players out of the hand—is used to win games. It is also used to obtain information and to mislead other players.

A player may bluff—continue to bet on a hand he knows he will lose—so that he can see his opponent's cards. This enables him to learn something about the other player's betting and bluffing behavior. Or he may bet on an obviously poor hand just to get the other players to misjudge his playing style.

So, part of poker is learning the skill of reading your opponents' behavior and keeping them guessing about yours. This means developing a "poker face"— no grinning when you peek at your cards and see you have two aces.

A poker game is a good vehicle for fidgety, restless adolescents and nervous adults to practice restraint from the tendency to drum fingers on the table, shuffle feet, or whistle when feeling tension.

Poker also provides an ideal situation for learning to look for cues in other people's behavior. Some adolescents, and indeed, some adults, cannot read the subtleties of behavior—facial expressions and body language—that signal that someone is worried, angry, or depressed. Watching fellow poker players for tell-tale signs is a good way to learn these important social cues.

Object of the Game

The object of Hold 'Em is to get the highest valued five-card hand, using any of seven cards: two "hole" cards (facedown cards dealt to each player) and five communal cards.

Equipment

A deck of cards; chips or tokens.

Value of Cards

Here are the hands, from highest to lowest.

Straight Flush   Five same-suit cards in sequence
Four of a Kind   Four cards of the same denomination
Full House   A pair and three of a kind
Flush   Five cards of the same suit
Straight   Five cards in sequence, regardless of suit

Three of a Kind   Three cards of the same denomination

Two Pairs   Four cards, with each set of twos being of the same denomination, such as a pair of eights and a pair of jacks

One Pair   Two cards of the same denomination, such as two threes

If none of the above are found in the game, then the hand with the highest card wins the hand.

If two or more players have pairs, etc., then the higher denominations are higher valued.

First of All

Players draw a card to determine the dealer. The high card deals the first hand. The deal then passes to the dealer's left. For authentic casino play, the dealer does not play the hand, and an indicator, called the *button*, is placed in front of each player in turn to announce that he is the dealer for that hand. A hockey puck makes a good button. Each player antes (bets on an agreed amount, say, one chip). Then the dealer deals each player two facedown cards.

Play

The player to the dealer's left must bet (that is, put in one or more chips). The other players, in turn, must choose to: *see the bet*—that is, put in an amount equal to the bet in order to stay in the game; *raise the bet*—in which case all players must equal that bet to stay in; or *fold*—go out of the hand, thereby forfeiting any chips or tokens already bet.

The dealer then deals three more cards faceup on the table. These are communal cards and are called the *flop*. Players bet again, this time calculating their strength on the basis of five cards. At this betting round players may *check*, that is, not bet any more chips but stay in the game. Of course, if one player bets, the others must at least "see" him to stay in the game.

Then a fourth communal card is dealt, followed by a round of betting. Finally, the dealer deals a fifth card. Players bet one more time (or fold) and then there is the showdown. The winner, the player with the highest valued hand, takes the chips.

Learning Skills
• learning to read facial cues and body language
• practicing self-control • calculating probabilities
• remembering the relative value of poker hands

♠♣ "Rule Number One: Always try to see your opponent's cards."—from a handbook on Scopa, a common Italian card game

Ages: 5 to adult
Players: any number

Object of the Game

The object of In Between is to bet correctly that the third card dealt will be in between the first two in numerical value.

Equipment

A deck of cards; chips or tokens.

First of All

One player is designated the dealer and does not get cards. Players take turns as dealer. Two cards are dealt to each player faceup.

Play

A player may *fold* (withdraw from betting) or bet. He bets that the number of the next card dealt will be in between the two numbers on the cards already faceup. The number of chips bet will reflect his confidence in his bet.

The farther apart the two cards are in value, the greater the probability of getting a card that is in between. If a player has bet correctly, the dealer must pay him the amount of his bet. Lost bets are collected by the dealer.

Learning Skills

• understanding concepts of "in between," "higher," and "lower" • calculating probabilities

Ages: 7 to adult
Players: best for 3

Black Maria is a very old game, dating back several centuries. It is relatively new to me, however. As a child I played Hearts, the game which must have evolved from Black Maria.

Object of the Game

The object of Black Maria is to avoid taking tricks that contain key cards.

Equipment

Deck of cards with the Two of Diamonds removed.

Point Value of Cards

The value of the cards is from ace, which is high, down to the 2, which is low.

These cards score against the player who takes them in.

Each Heart = 1 point
Ace of Spades = 7 points
King of Spades = 10 points
Queen of Spades = 13 points

First of All

Deal seventeen cards to each player. Before play begins, each player takes three cards from her hand—the cards she is most happy to get rid of—and passes them, facedown, to the player on her right. Players then add the cards they have received to their hands.

Play

The player to the dealer's left leads with any card. Players must follow suit. The highest card of the suit led takes in the trick, and the player who takes the trick leads to the next trick. If a player cannot follow suit, any card may be discarded. That, of course, is the player's chance to stick her opponents with cards that will count against them.

Scoring

Players' scores are the total of the cards that count against them. Play continues until one player reaches 100 (and is the loser). The player with the lowest score is the winner.

Learning Skills

• categorizing and counting • judging relative rank of numbers • considering several factors at once • mental flexibility • addition • reasoning • memory • calculating probabilities • developing strategies

ONE HUNDRED FIFTY

Ages: 8 to adult
Players: 2

Object of the Game

The object of One Hundred Fifty is to gain 150 points by taking in tricks and cards with point values.

Equipment

A 32-card deck (plus two jokers, optional). Remove twos, threes, fours, fives, and sixes from an ordinary deck.

First of All

Deal each player sixteen cards in two rows of four facedown cards, with one faceup card on each. If two jokers have been used, then deal the two remaining cards facedown as a "kitty." The nondealer may exchange any two cards in his hand for the kitty without looking at it first. If he doesn't want it, the dealer may exchange two cards for it.

Point Value of Cards

The cards equal their face value. Aces are high and jokers are the highest trump cards. Players can designate one as the smaller and the other as the larger. Here's the point value of the cards.

Ten = 10 points
King = 25 points
Last hand taken = 10 points

Bidding

The first player bids his estimate of the number of

points he will take in if he becomes the one to name trump. (Total points possible: four kings at 25 each, four tens at 10 each, and last hand for 10 points = 150 points.)

Bidding starts at 60. Players take turns bidding until one is unwilling to top his opponent's bid. The highest bidder names trump.

Play

The highest bidder leads the first card. Players must follow suit. If they cannot, they may trump. The trump card outranks all nontrumps. The highest card takes in the trick, and the player who takes the trick plays a card. As top cards are played, the card underneath is laid faceup.

If the player makes his bid, he is credited with his points. If he fails to make the bid, he goes "in the hole" by the total amount of his bid.

Thus, a player who bids 70 but only makes 60 is 70 in the hole, that is, -70. The opponent is credited with points taken in, in this case 90 ($150 - 60 = 90$). The first player to reach 150 is the winner.

Learning Skills

• categorizing • counting • estimating • calculating probabilities • judging relative value of numbers • developing strategies • addition (including negative numbers)

SIXTY-THREE

Object of the Game

The object of the game Sixty-Three is to be the first team to get to 200.

Equipment

Deck of fifty-two cards plus one Joker.

First of All

Deal nine cards to each player. Put the rest of the pack aside. Partners face each other.

Value of Cards

In play, cards have their face value with aces high and the Joker the low card, below a 2. The *opposite five* is the 5 of the same color as the trump cards. For example, if diamonds are trump, then the opposite 5 is the Five of Hearts. For scoring, here is the point value for trump cards taken in. The total point value is 63.

Ace = 1 point
King = 25 points
Jack = 1 point
Ten = 1 point
Nine = 9 points

Five = 5 points
Opposite Five = 5 points
Two = 1 point
Joker = 15 points

Play

After looking at their cards, players bid for the privilege of naming trump. The player to the dealer's left begins the bidding. The bid is the number of points the player estimates that he can make if he names trump. Bids are usually multiples of 5, but after 60, players can go as high as 63. The bid goes around until all pass except one player. When the bid is made, trump is named and players discard all cards except trump.

The successful bidder picks up the pack and deals cards to players so that they will have a total of 6. Then he plays a card which must be a trump. Players must follow suit if they can. The player who takes in the trick may lead in the following tricks. Play continues until the hand is finished. Partners then count up their points. If a player has not made his bid (counting both his and his partner's points), the amount of his bid is subtracted from his score. Opponents are credited with their own points.

Cards are dealt again, and the game continues until one pair reaches 200 points and is the winning team.

Tips for Good Play

Don't bid 63 unless you have the king, jack, and ten of the trump.

Try to work in cooperation with your partner, taking in valuable cards whenever possible. If your partner plays a valuable card, say a 5, and you can take it, do so.

Learning Skills

• calculating probabilities • estimating the value of a hand • working in cooperation with a partner • flexibility—distinguishing between a card's value in play and its value in scoring • keeping track of many variables

BEZIQUE

Ages: 8 to adult
Players: 2

Object of the Game

The object of Bezique is to earn points by taking in tricks that contain valuable cards or by laying down valuable combinations.

Equipment

Two decks of cards with the twos, threes, fours, fives, and sixes removed.

First of All

Deal eight cards to each player, dealing three at a time, then two, then three. Place the deck in the center of the table. Remove the top card and place it faceup at the bottom of the deck, sticking out for everyone to see. This determines trump.

Play

First player plays any card. Players do not have to follow suit except for the last eight tricks of the game. The highest card of the suit led, or the highest trump, takes in the trick. After a trick has been taken, each player picks a card from the stack so that there are always eight cards in a hand.

Players may lay down certain cards (see "Point Value of Cards") from their hand faceup in front of them. Even after they are placed faceup in front of a player, these cards are still part of the hand and are available for play. When the stack gets down to four cards (three facedown, one faceup), the winner of the trick gets one facedown card and the faceup trump card. The other player gets the remaining facedown two.

Play continues until one player gets 1,500 points and is the winner (about six times through the double deck).

Point Value of Cards

Each ace and ten that is taken in tricks counts 10 points. Here are the point-scoring combinations for layouts.

The Queen of Spades and Jack of Diamonds make bezique for 40 points. If, while these two cards are faceup, a second identical queen-and-jack pair is placed with them, that's double bezique for 400 points.

Four Aces = 80 points
Four Kings = 60 points
Four Queens = 40 points
Queen of Spades + Jack of Spades = 40 points
Four Jacks = 30 points
Four Tens = 20 points
Ten, Jack, Queen, King, and Ace of the Same Suit = 80 points

Learning Skills

• categorizing • judging relative value of numbers • memory • planning • counting • addition

SENTENCE RUMMY

Ages: 6 to adult
Players: 2 to 4

Object of the Game

The object of Sentence Rummy is to lay out cards in "sentences." In this game, cards have an alphabetical value, rather than a numerical one. Each card stands for the first letter of its name.

That means, ace = A, king = K, queen = Q, jack = J, two = T, three = T, four = F, etc.

First of All

Deal seven cards to each player, leaving the pack in the middle. Turn up the top card of the pack and place it beside the pack.

Play

As in other rummies, a player, at his turn, may take the turned-up card or the top card of the pack and must discard a card. At his turn, he may lay out a set of at least four cards, composing a sentence of the same number of words, each beginning with one of the card letters.

For example, the player lays down ace, king, four, and seven, saying "A kangaroo falls softly." Players may, at their turn, add to their own or another player's layout with a card that can be inserted or added to the sentence. For example, a player may place a 6 between the ace and the king in the above layout, saying "A short kangaroo falls softly."

For each card laid down, the player must pick a

card from the pack so that there are always seven cards in his hand.

Play continues until the deck is used up and the last layouts have been made.

Scoring

Layouts are scored as soon as they are made and the points recorded. A five-card sentence is worth 5 points. Adding a single card to make a six-card sentence earns that player 6 points.

The winner is the player with the highest score.

Here are some sample layouts and accompanying sentences.

Four—Queen—Two—Six—Seven:
"Father quit the Secret Service."

Eight—Three—Seven—Five—Six:
"Eat the soup for supper."

Learning Skills

• vocabulary • verbal fluency • grammatical awareness • phonic awareness

♥ When American astronauts orbited Earth, they took special fireproof playing cards with them.

ALLITERATION

Ages: 6 to 12
Players: 2 to 8

Object of the Game

The object of Alliteration is to win all the cards.

First of All

Deal six cards to each player. Players place cards in a facedown pile in front of them.

Play

The player to the dealer's left begins by saying, "I went to the department store and bought ..." As soon as he has said "bought," he turns over his top card to a central pile and continues by saying the number of the turned-up card and a noun that begins with the same letter as the number of the card.

For example, for a two he might say, "two tangerines"; for a four, "four firecrackers." For an ace, instead of "one," the player uses "an" and so might say, "an avocado." For face cards, no number is used, simply the first letter of the card. So, for a jack, the player might say, "a jellybean"; for a queen, "a quince"; and for a king, "a kite."

If the player continues his sentence correctly without hesitating, he takes in the card. If not, he leaves it there, to be taken in by the next player to win the top card.

Play continues this way until all the cards are played. The player with the most cards wins. If there is no winner, cards are dealt again. This time, players must precede the noun with an adjective (e.g., "five fine forks," "ten tiny turnips," "a queer quilt," etc.).

Variations

To encourage further vocabulary building, vary the carrier sentence: "I went to the zoo and saw . . ."; "I went to the toy store and bought . . ."

To elicit verbs instead of nouns, use this sentence: "My grandmother told me never to . . ." This can be made more difficult by requiring players to add two alliterative words—here, a verb and an adverb, or a verb and a noun. Children will begin to see the differences between verbs that are transitive (requiring an object) and those that are intransitive.

Some examples of sentences produced in this variation of the game follow. Two words finish the sentence. "My grandmother told me never to . . ."

Ace	act angry
Two	tease turtles
Three	throw tantrums
Four	faint foolishly
Five	fall fast
Six	swallow sardines
Seven	speak sarcastically
Eight	eat eels
Nine	nibble nuts
Ten	terrify tarantulas
Jack	joke jovially
Queen	quit quoting
King	kick kittens

Learning Skills

• practice in phonics (initial sounds of words) • verbal fluency • understanding of sentence structure and parts of speech • sensitivity to alliteration

Ages: 6 to adult
Players: 2

Object of the Game

The object of the game is to learn a concept—Coffee Pot—in as few trials as possible.

First of All

Each player picks a card. The player with the highest card is the "waiter." The other player is the "customer." The waiter decides on the definition of a coffee pot. This is a set of three cards with certain characteristics, e.g., all even, all of the same color, all under five.

Play

The waiter puts together several examples of "coffee pots" and "non-coffee pots" and shows them to the customer one at a time. The customer decides when he thinks he knows the definition, i.e., what makes a "coffee pot." The waiter then shows new examples and nonexamples, and the customer has to classify each as "coffee pot" or "non-coffee pot." The game continues until the customer has classified ten consecutive sets correctly. Then players switch roles.

Scoring

Players keep track of the number of examples the customer requires before he gets ten consecutive sets. This includes introductory examples as well as all correct and incorrect guesses that precede ten consecutive classifications. This number becomes the customer's score. At the end of an agreed number of rounds, the player with the lowest score is the winner.

Here is a sample game.

4—5—4   This is a coffee pot.
4—5—6   This is not a coffee pot.
5—5—4   This is a coffee pot.
2—3—10   This is a coffee pot.
2—2—3   This is a coffee pot.
2—2—4   This is not a coffee pot.
6—7—7   This is a coffee pot.

The customer announces readiness to be tested.
The waiter presents: A—A—A
The customer says, "not a coffee pot."
The waiter says, "wrong."
The customer asks for one more example.
The waiter presents this example: 10—10—3, advising, "This is a coffee pot."
The customer is ready again.

	Cards Presented	Customer's Guesses	Waiter's Responses
1.	2—3—10	Coffee pot	Right
2.	4—4—5	Coffee pot	Right
3.	4—4—2	No coffee pot	Right
4.	8—8—8	Coffee pot	Right
5.	A—A—4	No coffee pot	Right
6.	6—6—7	Coffee pot	Right
7.	9—9—A	No coffee pot	Right
8.	9—10—2	Coffee pot	Wrong
9.	5—5—4	Coffee pot	Right
10.	9—9—9	Coffee pot	Right

For readers who may not have figured it out, the definition of a *coffee pot* in this particular round was "a set with all numbers starting with the same letter."

Learning Skills

• deductive reasoning • classification • problem-solving

There are playing cards useful for travelers. Each card in the pack teaches a phrase in several foreign languages. In one deck, the Six of Diamonds gives the translation of "Where can I get a taxi?" in Spanish, French, and German: *"¿Donde puedo encontrar un taxi?" "Où est-ce que je peux trouver un taxi?" "Wo kann ich hier ein Taxi bekommen bitte?"*

A CARD PLAYER'S GLOSSARY

abbreviations   **P** = Player, **A** = Ace, **K** = King, **Q** = Queen, **J** = Jack

ace   usually the highest card in a deck, greater than a king in value. However, sometimes the ace counts as 1 point, the two as 2 points, etc. Its abbreviation is A. Each of the four suits—hearts, diamonds, spades, and clubs—has its ace, appropriately called the Ace of Hearts, etc. The ace has a single suit mark in the middle and an A in its corner.

ante   a poker stake (like a chip or token or two), usually put into the pot before the deal to build the pot

bet   put one or more chips or tokens into the pot (to "chip in") during a game. Players bet hoping to have a winning hand and to win the bet—and all the chips or tokens.

bid   At the beginning of some card games, players state how many tricks they think they can win. This statement is called a bid.

bluff   to try to deceive your opponent about the value of your hand in cards

button   an indicator placed in front of a player to signify that the particular player is the dealer. It is usually used in poker. Usually the dealer does not play that round.

call   to put in an equal number of chips or tokens (counters) as the previous bettor; to "see" the bet

check   In the card game poker, at the beginning of a round of betting, the first person who bets (the bettor) may "check," that is, bet nothing, but still stay in the game.

chip   usually a round disk or token used to make bets or "pay." Usually the player with the most chips at the end of the game wins. If you wish, chips may be exchanged for something of real value, like ten chips for not having to make a bed one morning.

clubs   one of the four suits, black in color, shaped like a clover

color   Hearts and diamonds are red. Spades and clubs are black.

court card   a jack, queen, or king; also known as a face card or royal card

cut   to divide the deck into two, not necessarily even, parts. This is used when the deck is shuffled and the stack on the bottom is put on the top. Also, each player initially, before the deck has been shuffled, may pick a card by "cutting" the deck and revealing the card to fellow players, to determine who deals the game.

deal   to give out cards to each player, according to the rules of the card game

dealer   the person who gives cards to the players; usually the dealer is determined by "cutting" the cards. The player who uncovers the highest card is the dealer.

deck   a complete set of cards (a pack); or unplayed cards

denomination   the number or face printed on a card. Two fours are cards of the same denomination, as are two queens or two kings, etc.

deuce   a two of any suit

diamonds   the red suit of cards with a diamond-shaped symbol on its face

discard pile   the pile of cards already played or rejected by players

draw a card   take a card from the stock

face card   a card with a face—a jack, queen, or king—from any suit; also called a royal card, picture card, or court card

facedown   only the backside of the card is visible, so that no one can determine its suit, denomination, or value

faceup   when a card is positioned so that it reveals the suit and number or value of the card

face value   the number of the card. The face value of a Two of Hearts or Two of Spades is 2 points, of any four 4 points, etc. Usually the royal cards have ascending point values, with the jack equal to 11 points, the queen 12 points, and the king 13 points. The ace is assigned 1 or 14 points, depending on the game.

flop   communal cards (cards everyone can share) laid faceup on the table

flush   five cards of the same suit

fold   withdraw from betting and go out of the hand, forfeiting any "money" already bet

four of a kind   four cards of the same denomination

full house   three of a kind (three cards of the same denomination) plus a pair (two cards of the same denomination)

hand   the cards a player holds in his hands; a round of a certain number of cards dealt each player

hearts   the red suit of cards with a heart-shaped symbol on its face

hole cards   facedown cards dealt to each player

"in the hole"   When a player fails to make his bid, the number of points of his original bid are deducted from his score. This means he is "in the hole." (See the game One Hundred Fifty, pp. 107–108.)

jack   one of the face cards or royal cards in a deck, represented in all four suits. Its abbreviation is J. A jack is higher than a ten and lower than a queen.

Joker   one or two extra cards supplied with a standard deck, which can be used in some card games as wild cards

kind   of the same value, like two tens or three fours

king   one of the face cards or royal cards in a deck, represented in each of the four suits. The abbreviation is K. A king is higher than a queen and usually lower than an ace (but see *ace*).

kitty   the pot

knock   to "go out" with a discarded card on the table, such as a nine. Then the player is said to be "knocking with a nine."

layout   cards presented on the table in a certain pattern, according to specified rules

leader   the card laid down or played first in a game

number cards   ace through ten

pack   a complete set of cards (deck); unplayed cards from which a player may draw a new card or from which the dealer may deal new cards to players; also called stock

pair   two cards of the same denomination

partner   a fellow player one teams up with in a given card game

pass   to surrender one's turn or refuse chips or cards

play   a given move or action taken by one player; also interaction between two or more players

player   person who is playing cards

playing cards   cards used in card games, as distinct from decorative or informative cards

points   number values assigned certain cards or accumulated by players in a given game

point value of cards   how much each card is worth, in assigned numbers or points. Point value may vary from one game to another, depending on the rules of the game.

poker   a card game with fixed rules which is played for chips or tokens (see Hold 'Em, pp. 100–103)

poker face   to adopt a kind of unreadable mask to prevent other players from guessing the value of your hand

pot   the collection of chips or tokens collected or won in a given game or series of games

queen   one of the face cards or royal cards in a deck, represented in all four suits. The abbreviation is Q. A queen is higher than a jack and lower than a king.

raise the bet   to add an amount to the original bet so that other players have to increase their bets to stay in the game

royal   a jack, queen, or king; also known as face card or court card

royal flush   a ten, jack, queen, king, and ace of the same suit

run of cards   three or more cards in sequence, like a four—five—six or a jack—queen—king

see the bet put in an amount equal to the previous players' bets in order to stay in the game

shuffle to mix cards, usually before a game, to make sure they are in random order. Among the kinds of shuffles people often use are the riffle shuffle and the overhand shuffle.

solitaire a card game one plays alone, effectively against oneself or the deck

spades a black suit of cards with a spadelike symbol

stack several cards on top of one another

stand pat not take any new cards

stock unplayed cards (the pack) from which a player may draw a new card or from which the dealer may deal new cards to players

straight five cards in sequence, regardless of suit. An ace may be high or low (follow or precede a king).

straight flush five cards in sequence of the same suit

suit cards belonging to any one of these four kinds: hearts, clubs, diamonds, or spades

Tarot deck a deck of 78 cards, including 22 pictorial cards. The suits were cups, wands, pentacles (or pentagrams), and swords. In medieval Europe they were used for fortune-telling as well as games. They are the ancestors of modern playing cards.

three of a kind three cards of the same denomination

token a chip or other small object, like a button, designated a certain value and used as payment to one player, given by another player or earned in a game

trump a suit chosen at the beginning of the game as having higher value than any other suit

two of a kind a pair; two cards of the same value, like two fives

value of cards the point value or other "facts" assigned to the cards in a given game

wild card a card that may assume any value, as needed in a given hand

About the Author

Margie Golick, Ph.D., is a professional psychologist, educational advisor, lecturer, and card shark living in Montreal, Quebec. She has an international reputation for her work with children and adults, specializing in learning skills and advising parents, teachers, and other professionals on ways to enhance learning for children with all levels of abilities.

Her special interest is developing methods and materials that entertain while they teach. She has helped children develop skills and problem-solving abilities that lead to greater academic success. She has developed educational kits, film strips, and computer software. Dr. Golick has published books helpful for both teachers and parents for using games in teaching, whether for learning-disabled or very bright kids. Her books include *Deal Me In!*, *Playing with Words*, and *Reading, Writing & Rummy*. With artist Jane Churchill, she produced the children's book *Wacky Word Games*.

Since 1975 she has been an advisor for CBC television's *Sesame Street* (now called *Sesame Park* in Canada) and serves as an educational consultant to several animated television series for children. She received a lifetime achievement award from the Alliance for Children and Television.

Dr. Golick is currently a consultant to Learning Associates of Montreal and chief psychologist of the Learning Associates of Montreal. Until 1990 she was chief psychologist at McGill–Montreal Children's Hospital Learning Centre, serving for over three decades. She has also been an educational consultant to the National Film Board, International Cinemedia Centre, Cinar Films, and Kutoka Interactive Software.

INDEX

What Is American Mensa?

American Mensa
The High IQ Society

One out of 50 people qualifies
for American Mensa . . .
Are YOU the One?

American Mensa, Ltd., is an organization for individuals who have one common trait: a score in the top two percent of the population on a standardized intelligence test. Over five million Americans are eligible for membership . . . you may be one of them.

Looking for intellectual stimulation?
You'll find a good "mental workout" in the *Mensa Bulletin,* our national magazine. Voice your opinion in the newsletter published by your local group. And attend activities and gatherings with fascinating programs and engaging conversation.

Looking for social interaction?
There's something happening on the Mensa calendar almost daily. These range from lectures to game nights to parties. Each year, there are over 40 regional gatherings and the Annual Gathering, where you can meet people, exchange ideas, and make interesting new friends.

Looking for others who share your special interest?
Whether your interest might be in computer gaming, Monty Python, or scuba, there's probably a Mensa Special Interest Group (SIG) for you. There are over 150 SIGs, which are started and maintained by members.

So, contact us today to receive a free brochure and application.

American Mensa, Ltd.
1229 Corporate Drive West
Arlington, TX 76006
(800) 66–MENSA
AmericanMensa@compuserve.com
http://www.us.mensa.org

If you don't live in the U.S. and would like to get in touch with your national Mensa, contact:

Mensa International
15 The Ivories
6–8 Northampton Street, Islington
London N1 2HY England